Elegy

For **BOB KAUFMAN**

NEELI CHERKOVSKI

SUN DOG PRESS
NORTHVILLE, MICHIGAN

ELEGY FOR BOB KAUFMAN

Cover design by Brian Schorn

Cover photo of Bob Kaufman © 1979 by Sue Kubly, courtesy of Eileen Kaufman

Special thanks to George Scrivani for editorial work on this manuscript. The publisher wishes to thank Judy Berlinski for her professional help in the preparation of this book.

Acknowledgments

Several of the poems in this book have appeared in the following journals:

Collision, Galley Sail Review, Tight
Would You Wear My Eyes: A Tribute to Bob Kaufman.
The Bob Kaufman Collective, S.F. 1987

Library of Congress Cataloging-in-Publication Data

Cherkovski, Neeli.
Elegy for Bob Kaufman / Neeli Cherkovski.
p. cm.
Includes bibliographical references.
ISBN 0-941543-13-7 (pbk. : alk. paper).—ISBN 0-941543-14-5 (signed pbk. : alk. paper)
1. Kaufman, Bob—Poetry. 2. Poets, American—California — San Francisco—Poetry. 3. Poets, American—20th century — Poetry. 4. San Francisco (Calif.)—poetry. 5. Beat generation—Poetry.
I. Title.
PS3553.H3534E44 1996
811′.54—dc21 96-47699
CIP

Printed in the United States of America First Edition

Elegy

For BOB KAUFMAN

ALSO BY NEELI CHERKOVSKI

POETRY

Don't Make a Move

The Waters Reborn

Public Notice

Love Proof

Clear Wind

Ways in the Wood

Animal

MEMOIR/BIOGRAPHY

Ferlinghetti: A Biography

Whitman's Wild Children

Hank: the Life of Charles Bukowski

revised edition, *Bukowski: A Life* (1997)

For Lisa Brinker and Kaye McDonough

INTRODUCTION

By Neeli Cherkovski

There always was Bob Kaufman . . . We walked into the Co-Existence Bagel Shop back in 1958—I was thirteen years of age—and there was the poet himself sitting across from Tiny Trent, an old hanger-on from the 30s, a guy named Mad Alex and several other North Beach regulars. Kaufman wore a light blue sports shirt, black trousers. His skin was smooth and he had a cup of coffee on the table before him. I knew he was a poet as my father's old friend Henri Lenoir pointed him out. Henri ran Vesuvio's across Adler Alley from City Lights Bookstore, one of the main watering holes. He had served drinks to Dylan Thomas, Jack Kerouac and more than half of the Beat Generation. And, of course to "Bomkauf" as well.

I wanted to meet him, but was reluctant to do so on my own. The only other poet I knew was a woman back home in San Bernardino who wrote sentimental rhyming poetry and published her own books in fancy hardback editions. At that time, I had just finished reading Lawrence Ferlinghetti's *A Coney Island of the Mind*, my introduction to modern poetry.

Our first encounter one on one took place seventeen years later. By that time I had read and re-read everything Bob had in print. The long poem "Second April," brought as much light into my mind as did Ginsberg's "Howl." Kaufman's poem, a defiant implosion of body mind soul cerebral cortex and Lascaux unbridled memories, brought the deep dark city jazz clubs and espresso bars into my head. Suddenly there I was, awake and walking in that extended vision of a churned-up America. Years after first reading it, Bob leaned over and whispered into my ear—as we watched "I Love Lucy" reruns on T.V. in the apartment we shared on Harwood Alley—"America does not love America." While I was thinking that one over, he raised his voice octaves to proclaim, "AND AMERICA DOES NOT KNOW AMERICA. . ."

Bob Kaufman is always on his way to second April. "O man in inner basement core of me." That is the continent of poetry. You'll find there Federico Garcia Lorca, T. S. Eliot, Wallace Stevens, Langston Hughes, and others who loom large in the Kaufman Kosmos. You'll enter many jazzy basements to encounter John Coltrane, Charlie Parker, Thelonious Monk and the topsy turvy comic Lord Buckley.

Impossible, but very real North Beach nights came rushing back to me when we took Bob Kaufman's ashes out on to San Francisco Bay one balmy afternoon . . . Lawrence Ferlinghetti, Jack Micheline, Parker Kaufman and myself. The old neighborhood seemed desolate without him.

He lived his life as a poet in the city, as a lover of jazz and hip language and a receiver of deep visions and graceful lyrics. Impossible wisdom fell into his lap and out of his fingertips. Lovely words formed on his lips. Bob Kaufman explained to me that I would never be lonely. The author of *Solitudes Crowded With Loneliness* said solitude was a ship on which we could sail far beyond the map of the known . . . He embraced me in Adler Alley (Kerouac Alley) and drew the tears of a failed relationship right out of me.

There was the night he read the whole of "Second April" at my wobbly kitchen table. Raymond Foye, Kirby Doyle, Howard Hart and myself . . . It was Bop City, Bebop City, the Five Spot, the Cellar, New Orleans, Chicago, St. Louis . . . It was Jelly Roll Morton, Louis Armstrong, lady sing the blues . . . And then, a few days later, he picked up my *Beatitude Anthology* and read: "Someone who I am is no one/Something I have done is nothing/Someplace I have been is nowhere/I am not me, What of the answers/I must find questions/All these strange streets/I must find cities for/Thank God for Beatniks."

Bob did not shy away from the title "Poet. Beatnik." He would die for poetry. He would tell the assembled habitués of the Caffè Trieste one morning, "Allen Ginsberg is king of the Beatniks." "The Ginz," sitting there reading the morning paper and drinking coffee, smiled and Bob came over to sit with him. But let's not be too romantic, and yet all is romantic enough. Praise Bobby Kaufman as he dances on the rooftops of paradise, beyond the veil. Old Bomkauf: "ABOMUNISTS DO NOT WRITE FOR MONEY; THEY WRITE THE MONEY ITSELF."

In 1978 I was picked up by the police for scotch-taping a poetry announcement on a utility pole. The cop shuffling me off to the paddy wagon was none other than Officer B____ who had harassed Kaufman in the Fifties. The self-proclaimed beatnik basher drove downtown, offering me a joint on the way. I refused, of course, and was placed into a holding tank of the county jail. When I was told I could make a phone call, I rang the Mayor's office where I got the Assistant Mayor on the line, an old pal from my political days. "We'll get you out," he told me with some amusement in his voice. I waited eight more hours for a fat deputy to come into the tank and ask me, "You the guy who called the Mayor?" "Well?" I answered. He led me down a corridor, had me sign some forms and then let me go down the elevator to the first floor. Who did I run into but Bob Kaufman, supported by two beefy cops on either side.

"Want me to wait for you?" I asked.

He told me to go on home and that he'd meet me later.

There was always Bob Kaufman, poet, and always his "Heavy Water Blues." "The radio is teaching my goldfish Jujitsu/I am in love with a skin-diver who sleeps underwater/My neighbors are drunken linguists and I speak butterfly . . ." Unique? You bet. And the humor . . . forever present. He used to joke with me over my love for young men. “I’ve got a new boy,” he’d say. “So beautiful. But I’m keeping him on the other side of town.”

Shortly after Bob’s death in January, 1986, I wrote what came to be “Elegy Eleven,” quickly followed by Elegy Twelve.” But several years passed before I wrote the remaining poems that came to comprise the present volume. They were not conceived as a book until mid-1994, when I suddenly realized how deeply Bob’s loss had affected me. At home, I sat at my desk and wrote. I brought the poet back to life and easily sensed his presence at my kitchen table, heard him again reciting poems, talking about jazz and the incidents of his early life. I read and re-read his books, dwelling especially on the classic poems “Walking Parker Home,” “Would You Wear My Eyes?” and “Bagel Shop Jazz.” Slowly the collection took shape. Living with this process taught me a lot about mourning, about the passing of a poet, and the loss of a certain constellation of bohemian life that will not come round again.

Outside of time, I wrote . . .

ELEGY ONE

I

Angelo the landlord
doesn't want Bob Kaufman's wiry ghost
wandering on his gyrating hallway's
Italian steps: "That man
is a crazy poet." Rozzelini's hawk eyes glow
as he lifts the broom
now warrior's lance aimed at the wall

II

I run to the streets
for reference
renowned windows shine
Rubicon eyelids flutter
people possess dreams of the Nile
my childhood song
fell into River Styx
conversation flows in the bayous
of our cluttered yards
we're tickled by distant snow

III

you might find Bob on a concrete raft

asking for a dollar,
he dreams sailing ships
across wide avenues
decked in Chinese banners

IV

cloud-driven choirs understand
blue jazz notes dripping like rain
we possess rippling walls
funny tears, Chaplin jokes
with which to cloak
nightly fear

V

Bob is 86'd from Vesuvio's
he yearns to redeem holocaust music
and epic haiku dances along the northern road
hierophantic somnambulists rise
to push single letters
onto his unfrozen brows, Adonis
enters the house of death
as he presses ten fingers
against clean glass

VI

Bob has a parade of rebels
tromping in his brain, they
sing Irish songs and ballads
of the the Abraham Lincoln Brigade
we dream of the Euphrates
and lift our arms
like doves
above sidewalk dreams

VII

Mister Kaufman has received a grant
from the National Endowment
they simply won't leave
him alone, it's fifteen
thousand dollars
cormorants nip his fingertips
wolves pursue his knees

VIII

the police never relaxed
around Bob, they shouted
with fists or billyclubs
one quiet coffee house afternoon
they picked me up, the next morning

they had Bob in tow
blood on his forehead, I grabbed
him, "Don't worry," he said, as they
pulled him away "I'll be home soon"
I left for Harwood Alley on the Third Street bus

IX

I saw the poet
wink at death in his serape
of purple bands
he held compassion
in his eyes and plenty of
sacred music on his lips
but he smoked and drank
then ran toward midnight
and hardly came home

when he died North Beach
took a dive
and didn't recover
bohemia
is a brittle
leaf
on a
tree

ELEGY TWO

I

every banner remains
in place, a frog hops through
narrow streets, big rats hide
famous windows wink
secretive, dead-end alleyways
embrace odd exile trembling
bearded ghosts, unbetrayed
eyes of Chinese postcards
tearful in the night, smile
we seize crackling wings
from passing clouds, hear
footsteps of people once
familiar, now gone
utterly blown-away
street names altered
in a twist of mind, miners
from the deep mines
turned dark butterfly yellow
a pilgrimage to the Far West
surrounded by trees, grass. water

II

St. Francis prostrates himself

before the Church of St. Francis
he is a rose bush
on a balcony near to our
favorite cafe
he invades our handsome
fear and aging streets

gulls crowd concrete
we're perched on
Telegraph, Russian
and Nob Hills

III

Bob's friend has been
taken away
to Laguna Honda Hospital
on the far side
of Twin Peaks to
whisper
beat melodies
against
dreaded
stone wall

IV

then Bob's face

disappears from
amused display windows
on Grant Avenue
intrepid artist, self-
portraitist, humorous
he is a lamppost
hugging Telegraph Hill
ghost boats enter the bay
with Chinese lanterns
masquerading as sea
gulls, tugboats embrace
our anonymous chambers
we descend into anemone rooms
spiraling toward magic doom
over death's commanding rose
we continue to shine

V

Bob returns
with Monsieur Apollinaire
they watch as Billy Holiday
enters the Co-Existence Bagel Shop
looking for an authentic
representative
of the Beat Generation

"Dying love, hidden in misty Bayous"

the piano
turns into a
horn, and divers
come up for tears
in time
to hear the poet
sing

"THE SUN IS A NEGRO.
THE MOTHER OF THE SUN IS A NEGRO"

FIFTY HORSES

I

fifty horses
over a ridge
like in a story
by Zane Grey

fifty horses
in town, close by
the towers of
finance and despair

we've lost our corner
Italian grocer, now
an empty window
faces us each day

fifty horses
with white manes
and brown
bodies, they

leap high
over the sun
and come along

the range

after the flood
and a great quake
fifty horses
all in my head

come running
past shuttered windows
to where
deep grass

closes in tightly
against rays
of night, one
hundred eyes

rise slowly, then
come floating
across a blue
swath of air

fifty Chinese musicians
cross Columbus Avenue
and play Italian
opera to their dead fans

the Chinese dragon

leaves Chinatown
and crosses to
our espresso cafes

fifty horses
made of bronze
sit on the shelf
in a curio shop

II

men rise
to build for
themselves
a horse

men die
to find within
themselves
a field, men

sing to
kill themselves
on horseback
and play

in green grass
when war

comes running
with brilliant

plans, men give
to the horse
magic, men
survive, horses

dive, they go
hurtling over
the edge
of history

ELEGY THREE

I

one day I told
a panther to step aside
so that I wouldn't succumb
but land on shore, I feel the need
to talk to one whose ashes
we tossed into water
during viper's reign

II

sometimes you step back
to hear another man's talk, maybe
you feel the woman in your body
or the animal in your desperation

you know a white rose
from a red one, a shattered window
from broken glass

III

seize proclamations
by invisible government, hear
imagination take off

for far islands, hear
crowds of pain call for
white waves

IV

“come love . . . sing a river . . .”
of dark fingers
and caresses, come sing
a bed and flowers, a window
half-ajar, the crowded kitchen
of manuscripts, books
music
and complaint

V

squalid arc of
hotel light broken
down by sound and sight
what immortal enemy
will meet my
animosity?

VI

New Orleans was
home one

wilderness ago
jazz crept up
the river
to his shoulder and he
shrugged, held
a pen and
wrote between
the notes

VII

believe in it
it's real
the bay
end of land
heron with
the sea
on his wings
ferryboat
winging
over the cold
current, past
Raccoon Straits
into the headland's
shadow

VIII

I speak like night
at Broadway and Columbus
frozen 7 PM
winter with big clumsy ice
out-of-sight Adonis
whispering
from window to window

IX

Sunday evening
alone on Grant Avenue
it's so late
my love has left
the bed is a crocodile
I cannot go home
not yet
I need to hang on
to glory
and solitary words

X

the past
comes in the room
like a parakeet

tiny beak, self-satisfied
ruffling of feathers
heart like
a human engine
of disbelief
when the candle
glows

XI

"come love . . . sing a river"
don't take the mystery away
not until I've nailed down
the night and slept
in sight of a perfect
rightness born
on the shifting sidewalks
of our neighborhood

A HARWOOD ALLEY ELEGY

I

alone
on Bob Kaufman
then Harwood Alley
transformed by
civic decree
near century's end
at six in the afternoon
reading Lorca's
Ode to Oblivion
better known
as the *Ode to*
Walt Whitman, a poem
Bob Kaufman
sang, splicing it
with Eliot or
Pound, Stevens
or Ginsberg

II

I look up
at number 28
where the man
and I sat

in a room
hammered out of
hard stone
pushing words
to the center
of a magic ring
as we felt ourselves
magicians

III

ruined
in time
taken down
the long
avenue
by silence
colliding
into silence
that ancient
dreamer
from the serpent's
tongue
old man
of ice flow
and ship's
prows, dawn
over the

water, he
recited
Hart Crane
to a roomful
of young
poets, we felt
"the chained
bay waters
liberty"

tongue for
tongue, word
for word, his
fingers
traced each stanza
in the air

IV

then one day
he suddenly
woke up
from his bed
and ran into
the kitchen, grabbed
my shirt
lapel and
gazed

into my eyes
with Langston Hughes
streaming
from between
his lips
rivers, rivers
and more rivers
until we arrived
at an imaginary
Nile on a raft
of single
letters

V

he left me
cold, silent
Lynne Wildey
called
to say
the poet
Bob Kaufman
had died
on a cloud
above
Coit Tower
and that
several gulls

were crying out
his name

long white
empty pages
of song, windows
on North Beach
cafe doors
swung open

we had a band
play innumerable
trombones
until his death
was some kind of
light, a feeling
for life
moving
toward
radiant
obliteration

VI

then it's every
wise wild
poet struggling
to be

reborn, I
read Bob's
moving lines

butterflies
in Whitman's beard
fly around
my eyes
and the lost
boys of Madrid
and the poor
boys of Havana
and the dark boys
of New York
and the cool boys
of San Francisco
all come to lean
against me

ELEGY FOUR

I

we were all a bit disturbed
maybe even crazy
some survived on Aid to the Disabled
others hobbled by
on odd jobs
there were bohemian mandarins
who wrote poems
published books
spoke out for saving the whales
and preserving peace

Bobby argued permanently
with outrageous authority
from every side of the social spectrum
he wrote himself into North Beach
as a blessed refuge
America was not quite right
yet even in the Beach there were shadows
of the Financial District leaning in

II

Bobby soldiered the dawn
he sometimes sat at a curbside

hoping to greet lions, leopards
or a Siberian tiger
maybe a herd of rhino
he slept
in Africa
and woke up
in New Zealand
Bobby sang the people
of San Francisco
he placed them in his poems
although you'd have to dig deep
in order to feel
their presence

his companions were out of whack
with the American Way of Life
call them dropouts
or street people
(they often lived there)

Bobby found his town
an exquisite maze
of simple facts such as
a fast escape to Chinatown eateries
or a quick exchange in the local park
glances meant to be imprinted
on the brain
he loved bars

cigarettes
and magic morning fog

by the time I knew him
he wrote very little
"it's all in my books
read my books"

III

remember
he was ancient
by age forty-five
by this I mean
that his skull
was wired together
by the terror of his
native land
and the sheer brutality
of forces
he could only think of
as dried bones
on the plains

Bob Kaufman
was a steam engine
he huffed and puffed
an engine with plenty of fuel

he went uphill all his days

IV

I ask friends
now
what is happening to
Bobby
on his way
to eternity
surely
he is not immortal
but we can
pull back the madness
and feel
the poet's clarity
the thing about poetry
is how it survives
and grows young
with time

Bob Kaufman
that Black Jewish
American was an ancient Celtic
priest
even, some say, an
Egyptian hierophant
could be he's the one who drew those animals

in the Lascaux caves
thousands of years ago

V

North Beach
has amusing
Italian arias and
young wide-eyed
wanderers reading
alchemical
past

Bob Kaufman
dove into words
on cold Saturday
afternoons. his eyes
a gateway, we found
in his work
the indelible stamp
of one who
ran through fields
of death
fire hands flaming
unconquered by
cruel dictionaries
or men robbed
of childhood

when he died
(a not unusual day
in San Francisco)
we hired a boat
and took his ashes
onto the Bay waters
looking back on San
Francisco and North
Beach, alive, reading
words in the air
feeling
the campfires
of a distant time
come nearer
hearing the horn
and the coyote
the bird's song

COIT TOWER

nostalgia is not what I'm
groping for; the light of Coit Tower
is merely a shadow in my head;
the gods whimper and fall, the saints
whisper and dive deep
into mutilated history;
unclear colors appear,
as quickly vanish; what I mean
is tomorrow and the endless sighting
of my eyes, what I need is you, again, old
companion of my brain, sensible,
nomadic, master of sidewalk, father
to storefront desire and mute
afternoon or deadening Sunday evening

Coit Tower rises over
North Beach; good
fortune rises in my daydreams;
memory became a rooftop
and the boundaries we set
for ourselves day-in, day-out,
the Tower is what you feel
and fear, it's how you flee
from yourself drinking coffee
unfolding a morning newspaper

the mind is what revels
in Autumn windows, you crack
the solemn walls open and find
uninterrupted time, perception
flows into a cupped hand,
friends disappear, ideas
go underground, emotions
run for cover, every death
rubs against the brain, you
hear tongues tremble and
walls fall into dust

you find the concrete tower
defying every pine cone
and all sequoia embanked
against the dreaded onslaught, your
kingdom is a ring
and the circle burns, Coit Tower
glows like a candle in pitch-black night, your
eyes observe clear rippling grass
of a song passed down
through the mind

where will you come, finally, to
sit? survival is one thing, but
self-knowledge without loathing
as the heart grows wider,
as the day of desire vanishes . . .

but when I think of Coit Tower
and the slope of Telegraph Hill
and the Bay water
my head is a fist
as night brings pride
to sit among us, how can I
rest? the idea is to become
anonymous, beatifically
silent, so no one can find you
in the still corner
of a cafe

ELEGY FIVE

I

read him,
Bob was a short, big-eyed
Black man, with sensuous lips, a noble
spirit, you have to
hear the dream he wrought
". . . in the inner basement core of me . . ."
the truth is I'm not yet fully reconciled
to his death or his life, Gregory Corso
said he had the biggest ego
in the Beat Generation, I say
he was maddening behind
a veil of crazy sainthood/I mean
the man sang, he wrote
clear jazz poems, clean childhood
memories that flow
into the delta land
deep elegies to Charlie Parker
and bumpy roads
into the arc of April

II

weep for all of us, we will
perish, our words will

someday fail us, they will
find a cemetery
where none should have been
coffins
buried with marigolds, anger
all gone, tragedy a simple
melody, Bob's
imagination
taught us about the bison
we keep killing
in our spiritual lives, the
Wounded Knees and
Little Big Horn betrayals
that make us not
quite complete

III

weep for eucalyptus
dying up and down the coast, for
fog over Twin Peaks
poet invader
come to tell us
our plagues work from within
we hear the cop coming down on poets
in the 1950s, a brute
I met years later, with huge
unpoetic grimace and

massive hands
how Bob elbowed into silence
when Kennedy was killed
how the prisoners
weep for a song
and have no one
to sing for them

IV

read him,
lift a book into your eyes
this man fled into America, right
into the cyclone, he didn't
fear vast armies, nor
turn from amazing light, he lit
saddened rooms with rhythmic
silence, his friends
talked of him
as if he were a mountain
some said
Bob Kaufman
ran like a river
from the heights
to a flat plain

V

tell him
you can hear the bison herds
make him hear
his own words
let him read to you
from the white page in
living print, this poet
born in New Orleans,
gone to New York, then
west to California,
take the poet
into your arms
and let him
rage or
wander, a silent
spirit
a guiding
hand,
a light in the
field

VI

he used to wander
on Grant Avenue, his
neighborhood, an old Italian

refuge in San Francisco, people
heard his eyes, they
said Bob was an entire
mountain range, dumfounded
voices found space
inside of his own
wise vision
Bob
knew the buried
heroes of America
who no one else knew
men and women destined
for thin-walled rooms
and dingy hallways, people
who often lived
on the streets
jazz trumpeters and
lost balladeers
clinging to the poet's
severe gentleness

VII

but I'm born to hear his voice
and to realize
my own, to feel my way
across America, to take
the memory of this man

in hand and fling it
over the burning heads
of the city, to say
this was a poet
taller than redwood, leaner
than time, able
to feel his way
along the body of our coast, to
say there's continuity
in making the land
into a poem,
to actualize love
of land in
knowledge of the hand
and body, to whisper
a song through the dangerous
world and
become more than
a mountain

VIII

no matter what I say
the man is gone
so read him
let wind
flow through your fingertips
take indifferent roads

make them sisters
surrounding sky
your brother
wicked trees
your secret lovers
every canyon
shelter
condors
revived
bison herds
returned

be patient
with anger, your
natural fear
wheels
turn on the
hearse and
the cop
brings his club
down like an afternoon
shower

IX

we descend
only to rise once more
weep for your

sister
who is silent, take
your brother's hand
across the wide lawn
this place where Indians dreamed
now calls
for your understanding
a simple flower
may tell you
complex things, and
endless
discourse may rise
out of your
private requiem

here is an elegy
clear as light
cruising the coast
Bob
was an avalanche, he
darted in and out
of the tall trees, took
my hand in his
saw dead faces and
heard the voices
of conspirators
racing across clouds

what I feel
is his death, and his
life, he was a sprite
and a warrior, a wounded
man and a
complete vision, "Second April"
was the poem
he wrote
expressing drug reality
and red jazz nights

X

read him, that's how you find
your comfort, commune
with the good order
of art, take
the land in hand
and find it
as your mirror
this man
came from the South
rode subways
and organized
workers
on the waterfront
we used to walk
along San Francisco's Embarcadero

way back then, singing
old Commie songs, sentimental . . .
he'd smile
inside, he'd show brown
crooked teeth and big
gaps in his mouth
and clear, wide eyes and a fist
of words

XI

I am the one
who will mourn
my companion dies
in my hands
my friend awakens
to die
he lives
in this continual
death

we were able to amaze
ourselves
back in the 70s when
we first met
already he was the famous beatnik
poet
his serape

and cool
shades, his
trembling hands
and bottle of
beer, his need
for a handout, for
the memory
of April
rising
from inside

XII

someday
it will be said
the poet grew
into nothing less
than silence, like
what you encounter
on a cliff at
sunset after a storm
a silence
for the gods
a sadness
rushing toward
continual joy

Bobby was an animal

pacing
the page, he pushed
the dream
a little further
he added fire
to the flame
he bowed his head
in a band leader's hat
and closed his eyes
sadly

Bob Kaufman
lit up the kitchen
in my apartment
at Harwood Alley, tipping
a bottle over and
standing on a chair, then
suddenly he stared
at me straight in the eyes
wearing a straw hat
as I gathered his ashes
and fed them to the Bay

XIII

read him,
tell me that the words
glow

hear waves
intimate and
cold, easing
onto shore
or the echo
of waves
or the idea
of waves, a lone gull
and a long
distant voice
streaming
out of the
void

ELEGY SIX

when I said
Bob Kaufman
had become
a box of trinkets
I should
have said
a wheel of
magic, that he
had turned into
a beatific
language
of slam-bang
music, that
he had seen
rain overwhelm
pure blossoms
of understanding
and compassion

faces used to turn
his way
in dark-lit bars
with gangplanks
that led
to crude sorrow
and

into the resolute
circus
of an ironic gaze

Bob Kaufman
wore perpetual
rivers in his
head, he
was, nevertheless,
a man with
the common
voice, a funny
and tragic
figure who
knew the
sacred fool
and doomed
companion
of a hangman's
noose

his passionate
and determined eyes
never reproached
the street
trumpeter
but sang
every note

from the
sidewalk
mines of
rebellion

WITH THE LUCK
OF A NATURAL
POET, ONE WHO
TOUCHED THE
SLOPING FIELD OF
VOICES, THE
GNARLED HAND
OF OAK TREES
AND REDWOOD
EMANATIONS,
HE CAME DOWN
THE HILLSIDES
AND ENTERED
EVERY OPEN
HEART JUST
LIKE A JET
OF LIGHT
IN THE MORNING

some days
death isn't
death

life is a green
riverbank
where the
listener
will not
be defeated
all-consuming
fire
lifts us
high
above animosity
into
a beam of
flame

the candle
of a third
eye in
our primate
head

there the man
reads rapidly
from the brick
walls
steel beams
and store
windows

improvised music
of the spoken
word

understand
this man
and
his plan
for "Second
April" everyday
of the year
his pictures
of a sardine plainly alive
in our lives
ruled by fate
and by a drummer's
precision
at the dawn
of time

when I said
Bob Kaufman
I meant the
poet, he lived
in San Francisco
during the
Beat Generation
and died many

years later
from the onrushing
crush of
angels who
were neither
cruel nor
envious
but truly
able to
fly

ELEGY OUT OF SEQUENCE

For Eileen Kaufman

now comes the madrigal
for Mister Kaufman
as I sit
in Caffè Trieste
a wounded cobra
my fangs
of glass
work toward
happiness but
despair and
death seem to plague
their way

oh for a moment
of restless rest
with coffee gods
clanging
their cymbals
across the wide
avenue
to this side street
with its
church doors shut
and phantom
street musicians

lost for
good

Bob Kaufman
can you
return
with brocaded coat
a captain
of song
for sure
as I sit
with your wife
Eileen
who informs me
we're coming back
she says
there's a group
reincarnation
yes
that means
Bob Seder and
his jazz trombone
and that means
Captain Jack
with crushed in
mug and
that means
Big Mike

the Fence
and Crazy
Alix
and Tiny Trent
and the Irish
painter who danced
on table tops

that means
everyone
returns for
one last jig
and one last
all-nite party
with every possible
drink drug

even Rumi
and Villon, Rimbaud,
Baudelaire,
Lorca, Eliot,
Verlaine, all
come to be
in our
spirit ballet
so says
Eileen
across the table

from where you
sat some time
ago

I hear the espresso
machine hissing
and seize
the moment
for my own
dervish dream
of endless
poetry
and an end
to servitude
behind register
or desk

we lived
in a palace
of Chinese
food and
Italian cafe
afternoons
and we live on
and on

now it's *Cranial*
Guitar handed

to me
wherein
the city is
“a beautiful
jealous bitch”
in which we
abide

on the second
day of April
in the Caffè Trieste
four years
until the millennium
spreads wing
and soars
toward
a reincarnated
dream

ELEGY SEVEN

I

Bob on the Bayou, one foot in front
of a frog, a man with a frog's face
passes, leaping, a man with a frozen heart
tries to talk, this world
is hot and the air burns

"Bob was always
a poet. you just knew it"

II

sweet descending chariot
every turn of the wheel
is a parting of the lips
painful night slips away toward
dawn/night can be intolerable, the crickets
and untrammeled darkness folded over darkness

III

he would tell us, years later
not so much of the Bayou as it was, but
as he imagined it still to be
whispered "fire" telling me of a great fire

faraway, "in a dream" he said, like fireflies
or fear leaping over a fence

there was a mangy dog on the corner
Bob's father read books, his mother
gave him that faraway look, dreaming
of green hills in Martinique

IV

Bob remembered people talking of
war and peace, later he wrote that "the men
who died in previous wars became popes and presidents"

V

as a child there were long moonlit
nights, the white man in Bob's body
used to pass like a low-lying cloud.
the Black Man wore a guitar,
he sang for his lost
mother one languid
night, I was there, I heard
sweet chariot ascending. the light
of young eyes alive, he heard a word
like stone drop onto stone and his ears
never stopped ringing

VI

wait and you'll be surrounded
wait awhile and you might hear
give desire a chance and peace
will come tearing into your ears

Bob saw America
bend to the song of invisible people
on the land

his childhood sailed away
along the Mississippi
onto a merchant ship
bound for New York

VII

the South held him a fleeting moment,
then John Coltrane ran through his fingers
and up his arms. he'd sit for hours
inventing these United States of Desire

VIII

there were blue doors in the North which
he opened onto the prison of liberty's shadow

Bob knew that his childhood
was a hand mirror inside of him

ELEGY EIGHT

I

so many people
talk of knowing Bob
Kaufman, this
live-wire in the
heavy duty
bars, this man
of April with
wife Eileen who
typed the
poems Bob threw into
the air

love, anger
the pain
inside of
floral wreaths, his
slender hands capable
of wringing
the night

II

unhateful
street corners

where even
fog
sat in the dives
drinking
or ordered
chop suey
in a basement cafe
on Jackson Street
before the
plague

III

just loud
enough
a whistle
and he
came

expounding
on poetry
of the Beat
Generation
he said,
"Allen Ginsberg
is king . . ."

clearly
he believed
poetry
a ring
you wore
in your
deep
desire

IV

"there is no
third world,
there are
many worlds,"
said Bob
Kaufman on a
political night
around the wobbly
table at
28 Harwood
Alley

V

he held his fingers
high and read

"Second April" from beginning
to end as we listened
to the closing of a wound

ELEGY NINE

I

his anger
is felt
but you have to brush aside
the words
much as you'd do to tall grass
on the shoreline,
anger like a blade
coming down on the angel
of memory, what is this man
and who does he remember?
an acacia or dried roses
scattered
everywhere, Bob
came to the park
with a limitless song, he
saw the tides within a man's head
and pushed hard
as the sun toppled

II

in jail
Bobby saw the sacred land, he
fell for it, "thank God

for Beatniks"
meaning,
I believe, a forest of people
seeking to resist the murder
of imagination, the packaged
sensibility, the lack
of feeling, the need to
be violent, the desire
to be a real man, the need
to see a woman
go down on her knees
he could be angry with Moses
but he felt deeply
for the death
of a flower
in the death
camps

III

Bob's anger
is mine.
you can take
it also
we have
imprisoned
America
We have

clubbed
America
take any bit
of land and see
how it
bleeds

IV

Bobby used to come in
to the place we shared
with a few beers, he'd
sit at the table, I'd want
to hear a new poem a piece
of an old one, but he
mostly stared
at the wall, then
he would turn
and talk about sorrow or
solitude, and in this
talk great joy
grew, I'd feel
renewed, I can't
explain it
any other way

V

Ancient Rain
I address
this angry note
to you —
old lean
Black bison,
your shaggy spirit
makes me want to
fly to where
I know you are
walking, to feel
what you must
be feeling
old bent
body down
in bed, I used
to count the
days that dropped
around us, you
were dying
and we knew it

A GRANT AVENUE ELEGY

I

we were a sight
in the Caffè Trieste
back in 1975 and the years
that followed, time
never guillotined us
and we remained
sure of
our beat
attitude
right up
until the doors
shut
for the night

hand to
hand, eye
to finger, luck
and ambition
conspiring
into a single
song

II

I despaired
of being
anything more
than a shadow
in a corner of the cafe
slanted caps
of poetry kept the past
alive, dreams
drunken reveries
on mystical sidewalks
faraway

III

how often the captain
wandered back and
forth on Grant Avenue
his slight frame
and wiry eyes
awake to every voice
that called
from shop windows
and fog-bound air, he
answered fallen gods
and gave a hand
to angelic choirs

struggling to be
reborn

IV

moving like music
in a jazz
combo he
continued
writing silence
onto twilight
requiems, he
lived in many
secret hotels
and drank alone
in quiet Chinatown
bars, his eyes
saw Lao Tzu on
a streetcorner
alive
one single
Coltrane
note
reverberating

V

he never became

an old man
this merchant marine
organizing
New Orleans born
Grant Avenue
patriot
for poesy, but sat
in a chair
across from
the espresso bar
tapping fingers
on the table
demanding
red faces
and red wings
and tall
birds
flying
beyond the doom
of frozen windows

VI

we were
born for the low-lying
wooden buildings
and those
aged Italian

delis and
hardware stores, Coffee Gallery
odors and
swift-moving
lips
of voices
passing

this was
our wild west
and yellow wood
endless smoke
and caffeine air
and conversations
every possible
ribald poem
and singable elegy
ribbons of darkness
and river run

against the ruins
of time

ELEGY TEN

I

Hey, poet, amigo, that's me again and I guess
if you are dead these streets are a shipwreck
I move from within/your brown
New Orleans body, you sat
in the kitchen alone, you fell for it
someday I'm going to fall
on your hands and you'll scream
you were the last real
beatnik old blood, your father rumored
to be a rabbi, your mother
from Martinique, I guess life and
time fall on their knees, I suppose
there's a generation filled with sorrow
waiting behind the door, I think
ribbons of blood fly like birds
in my head, when we tossed you
into the sea your ashes
went into my head, old beatnik, hey
Old Rain, that's meat, real live
red meat, that's you joking a turban
on your head a jazz combo
in your feet a piece of Lorca
like a river on your eyes a
bit of Eliot in "Prufrock"

singing a ghost of Bayou
Saint John your childhood
haunts, I guess what I'm writing
is America, the ghost flows
the river feeds us from the mud, we go down

II

I thought I saw The Ancient Rain
alive on Grant Avenue, I saw
my friend again, roommate
old buddy, I said
it was all over, told him
in a poem that I loved him and felt
pissed off, really, he dominated
the saints of Caffè Trieste, he rode herd
over silence in the place we shared
now a renamed Harwood Alley, what a joke
of monument we become, every plan
for anonymity just keeps getting
ripped-off by people
who need to apologize
for their civic unrest/they
throw people into the streets, they
throw them onto Kerouac Alley and
Saroyan Place and now into your
face old Bob. we used to climb
drunk those crazy stairs

in Angelo Rozzelini's building
he'd call me to say "you keep
the crazy poet in your place . . .
he gets drunk all the time and messes
up the place . . ."
Mrs. Rozzelini took me aside, "Angelo,
is plenty mad . . ."
but you stayed six months,
your wild hair, you Van Gogh eyes, your
Federico Garcia Lorca tongue, your
New Orleans arms, your rabbinical shuffling

III

I saw the real live ghost
of "Second April," I saw
John Coltrane leaning
out of a window and
Charlie Bird Parker
walking into my kitchen
and Lady Blue
and all those others
who knew you, your brother
showing up one day, heavyset
dressed in a suit, looking
for his disorderly brother
the beatnik poet as he called
him . . . sure, that's my

man, you can kiss
his fingertips, you can
touch his fluttering eyes
it's America we're running
up against, an avalanche maybe
of used tires and
condoms, a gang of
kids who never heard the man
sing. you better believe it
'cause it's coming your way
jazz and poems, the
struggle of a black hand
on a dark guitar, of a pair
of lips on
a trombone, of a river
inside of the body, of a
gloved hand
shaping a poem
he read
Langston Hughes
as the kitchen table
shook, did he ever pay
any of the rent? I bought
dinner and beer
he came home to read
Nile and Euphrates, and
to sing mountain and
valley, a city

poet, to tell me
I could never be
alone. then one day
we argued over a poem
he was drunk out of his
mind and I had smoked a
lot of hash, but the problem
was the poem looming
so large, pouring over
the remains of the beat
generation and its afterglow
picking us up
in its swirl of words
and silent spaces . . .
I have seen a man
like him before
Kaufman, you
have the volcano
in your head, you shook
the poem onto the floor
it was yours, it was
mine, it flooded us with
grief and then unimaginable
joy, you were an old Commie
in the Merchant Marines
as a young man
you sat around the jazz clubs
in New York City and

then you headed west, oh
I met your elegant sisters
from down South, poised
red handbags, and
did we sing, you and
I, "The Love Song
of J. Alfred Prufrock" and "Ode to
Walt Whitman" rang
through the three rooms
at Harwood Alley
and jumped onto the
street

IV

that's your merchant of power
on the street and
the future homeless
dazed veterans and those who resisted
who read *Golden Sardine*, each poem
a weapon against
murder on the streets

that's my friend
everyday, blue bandanna round
his head, eyes shining, slender
body wracked, his wild
walk, we feel on instinct

what to do next, to rip
the poem from the air
and nail it onto paper

ELEGY ELEVEN

I

from out of the Tempest
he came
like Ariel

running,
he braves
his ashes

and lights
a two-headed candle
in the room

on chimeras,
each petal
on the flower
in his hand

is free to speak
bird, bee
philosophy

a stream
liberated from
Bayou

wild in the text
of a singular
day

II

he left for good
early Sunday morning
not quite aware

of the crowds
who were arriving
hoping to explain

themselves to
his words,
unvanquished

he never forgot
who he was:
Bob Kaufman, Poet

III

he peeked into a keyhole
and saw
Orpheus sitting at the bar
dreaming, orating,

he transformed
an entire neighborhood

in his own words
we heard keen
anthology

at work, Oh
where do you ride?
faster and faster

into a mine-shaft
filled with
a guessing-game

a dance
and an open door
for song

IV

far from the art
of poetry
he gathered

an ark
of words
and placed them

together
so that they were
not unlike

a wild, rock-strewn
coastline
battered and admired

night and day
by equally
feverish waves

V

we lived together
for some time
in a ship

of silence
sleeping
where the dazed

streets
were more
Xanadu

than California,
that is

part of the miraculous

wave
we knew
and know

there he is
gone
there are

at least
his words
from the Gulf Stream

waters
he sailed
to become
a sailor
recognized
as our own

VI

the evasions
in his work
are invaders
from outside,
he had

the heart

of a warrior
he invited
every mirror

to look
deep into
placid pools

and turbulent
magic
waters

his hands
when reading
often encircled
the world
there were years
when he hardly
spoke or
wrote
some days

exhausted
he came in
the door

and recognized
another door
no one else

could see
through that door
he entered
sleepless
remembrances
thwarted by his

body
he came home
sweet-

faced, solitary
strong,
and hard

January 12, 1986

ROOTS

it matters when you tear bark
off a neighborhood tree
revealing gossip elegies
buried beneath rubble
it matters when you pass
ghost butcher shop
dead meaty hands
grumble of butcher
in green smock
eyes like a pit bull's eyes
greasy mouth
howling silence

we demand another man's wrath
to fall, rain surrounded
by wrecked pavilions, javelin
cracked, blown through the Gate
by dust, remains of one life
snuffed out
hanged man made right
words torn to smithereens
by skeleton orchestras
the 'other man's' rage

we're returning to the neighborhood
late morning, police have snatched

one side of Vallejo Street
near Church of Saint Francis
on whose steps a statue of the saint
stood until pelicans ate
the stone before sunrise

there are ponies waiting
to be driven over cliffs at Land's End,
it's the repetition
of a hard note, jazz clarinet
affixed to American hands
as landlords
are consigned to South City rest homes:
Haven Hill, Raven's Nest

Washington Square Park
flies toward the Great Wall of China
battlements intact, hordes
spin, windows shine

scribble mercy past cigarette night
Kerry Dancers sing Italian arias
Mister Puccini and Mister Verdi
walk into a cafe looking for beatniks
and failed dreamers, they burrow into
cracks, they inhabit
lost video artists and puppeteers who perform
before vanquished thrones, on Broadway

magazine racks are invaded by Asian-American
teenagers, glued to the sex mags

a circus of performing elephants
zooms over flame-flanked rooftops
until the fat lady throws down the gauntlet, we
are a fiery table of espresso noise
and self-congratulatory fire

ELEGY TWELVE

I wanted to cry
but I saw your ashes.
Ashes.
I wanted to laugh
but I saw your ashes.
Cry.
I wanted to ask
but your ashes laughed.
Ashes.
I needed to be as gray
as your ashes, as vulnerable
and alone.
Cry.
I needed to throw
your ashes
away.
Laughing.
I wanted to toss
your ashes right then.

I held the box in my hand
and saw your son
wave good-bye
as over the side of the boat
you dove.
Ashes.

I sprinkled your ashes
into the wind.
I saw the sun
leap like a whale.
I heard foghorns
bleat for love.
Ashes. Ashes.

I fell to the side
of my tears.
Laughing.
I tossed your tongue
onto waves.
Laughing.
I tossed your cigarettes
into the brink.
Alone.
I said how cheap you were
when I asked for a loan.
You, with government grant
and monthly welfare check.
Big saint.
Ashes.
Cry.
I tossed ashes
into your eyes.
Laughing
I threw my body

into your ashes.
Alone.
I gave your fingers
to a storm
and passed your ashes
to another.
Crying.
I saw tears in Neptune's
eye
and gave ashes
to clouds.
Passing.

I turned your ashes
into bone, your spirit
into flesh.
Living.
I saw your ashes disappear
into water.
Alone.

ABOUT THE AUTHOR

Neeli Cherkovski was born in Santa Monica, California in 1945. He attended California State University in Los Angeles, earning a B.A. in American Studies, and spent two years at the Hebrew Union College-Jewish Institute of Religion, also in Los Angeles. Cherkovski moved to San Francisco, California in 1975, where he edited "Beatitude," a poetry magazine founded by Bob Kaufman and Allen Ginsberg. In the same year two of his poetry collections were published, *The Waters Reborn* and *Public Notice*. In 1980, *Love Proof: Poems and Drawings* appeared, followed by *Clear Wind* in 1983.

In 1979, Cherkovski's *Ferlinghetti: A Biography* was published, one of the first important Beat Generation studies. His ground-breaking collection of critical memoirs, *Whitman's Wild Children,* came out in 1988. It has become a standard handbook for students of contemporary poetry and Beat literature. In 1991, Cherkovski's life of Charles Bukowski, *Hank,* was published to wide critical acclaim.

Animal, a new collection of poetry, appeared early in 1996 from Pantograph Press.

Photo: Steve Wilson 1994

Printed for Sun Dog Press in November 1996.
1000 copies were bound in paper wrappers of
which 126 copies are numbered & signed
by the author.